A LOOK AT PRIMARY SOURCES

AUTOBIOGRAPHIES

BY KRISTEN RAJCZAK NELSON

Gareth Stevens
PUBLISHING

CRASHCOURSE

Please visit our website, www.garethstevens.com. For a free color catalog of all our high-quality books, call toll free 1-800-542-2595 or fax 1-877-542-2596.

Library of Congress Cataloging-in-Publication Data

Names: Rajczak Nelson, Kristen, author.
Title: Autobiographies / Kristen Rajczak Nelson.
Description: Buffalo, New York : Gareth Stevens Publishing, [2024] | Series: A look at primary sources | Includes index.
Identifiers: LCCN 2023001180 (print) | LCCN 2023001181 (ebook) | ISBN 9781538287477 (library binding) | ISBN 9781538287460 (paperback) | ISBN 9781538287484 (ebook)
Subjects: LCSH: Autobiographies--Juvenile literature.
Classification: LCC CT25 .R354 2024 (print) | LCC CT25 (ebook) | DDC 808.06/692--dc23/eng/20230124
LC record available at https://lccn.loc.gov/2023001180
LC ebook record available at https://lccn.loc.gov/2023001181

First Edition

Published in 2024 by
Gareth Stevens Publishing
2544 Clinton Street
Buffalo, NY 14224

Designer: Claire Wrazin
Editor: Kristen Rajczak Nelson

Photo credits: Cover (photo) Irzhanova Asel/Shutterstock.com; series art (background texture) Verbena/Shutterstock.com; series art (cover typeface) Gleb Guralnyk/Shutterstock.com; series art (photo frame) Nataliia K/Shutterstock.com; p. 5 (top) Andrzej Sowa/Shutterstock.com; p. 5 (newspapers) Copyright Lawrey/Shutterstock.com; p. 5 (antique photo) Elzbieta Sekowska/Shutterstock.com; p. 7 Ivan Kruk/Shutterstock.com; p. 9 (portrait) vkilikov/Shutterstock.com; p. 9 (autobiography page) File:Autobiography_of_Benjamin_Franklin_with_his_essays_and_will_(1900)_(14778459312).jpg/Wikimedia Commons; p. 11 Everett Collection/Shutterstock.com; p. 13 Joseph Sohm/Shutterstock.com; p. 15 Kathy Hutchins/Shutterstock.com; p. 17 File:23_May_18_047_(42273332192).jpg/Wikimedia Commons; p. 19 (headshot) File:AlmaFlorAdaHeadshot.jpg/Wikimedia Commons; p. 19 (books) Peter Kniez/Shutterstock.com; p. 21 VisualArtStudio/Shutterstock.com; p. 23 (top) sweeann/Shutterstock.com; p. 23 (headshot) File:Anne_Frank_passport_photo,_May_1942.jpg/Wikimedia Commons; p. 23 (writing in diary) Tatiana Popova/Shutterstock.com; p. 25 File:Katherine_Johnson_at_NASA,_in_1966.jpg/Wikimedia Commons; p. 27 File:From_the_ballet_Coppelia.jpg/Wikimedia Commons; p. 29 REUTERS/Alamy Stock Photo

Printed in the United States of America

Some of the images in this book illustrate individuals who are models. The depictions do not imply actual situations or events.

CPSIA compliance information: Batch #CS24GS: For further information contact Gareth Stevens at 1-800-542-2595.

CONTENTS

Words in the glossary appear in **bold** type the first time they are used in the text.

THE FIRST SOURCE

Every day, people create primary sources. These are firsthand accounts of **events** that happened. Autobiographies are one kind of primary source. They can teach us about people's lives and where and when they lived.

MAKE THE GRADE

Other primary sources include letters, artwork, photographs, and newspapers.

TELLING THEIR STORY

An autobiography is a book about a person's life written by that person. It is written from their **point of view**. The **author** may have **witnessed** a notable event or time period in history. They may have lived an interesting life.

MAKE THE GRADE

A biography is a book an author writes about someone else's life.

EARLY AUTOBIOGRAPHIES

The first autobiographies were written around the 15th century. In 1791, Benjamin Franklin's *Autobiography* was published, or put out in book form. It became the first widely read autobiography. Franklin told the story of his life as well as gave readers advice, or suggestions, on what to do.

MAKE THE GRADE

It took Franklin almost 20 years to write his autobiography.

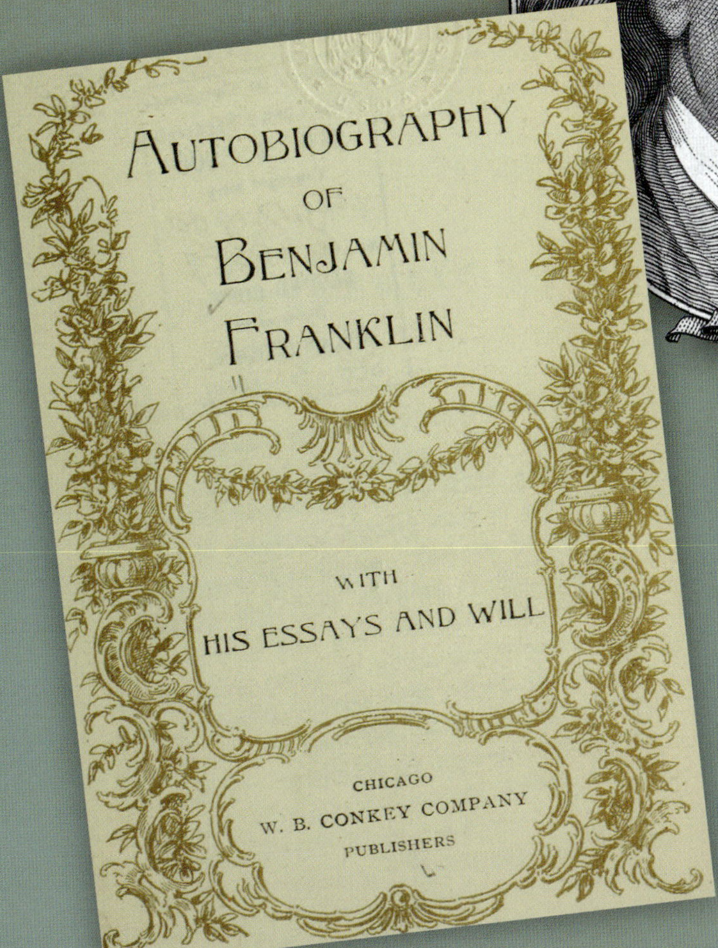

AUTOBIOGRAPHY
OF
BENJAMIN
FRANKLIN

WITH
HIS ESSAYS AND WILL

CHICAGO
W. B. CONKEY COMPANY
PUBLISHERS

FEATURES OF AUTOBIOGRAPHIES

Autobiographies are always written using first-person pronouns, such as "me" and "I." A **traditional** autobiography is written when the author is older. They are looking back at their whole life. Autobiographies have many personal **details** only the author would know.

FREDERICK DOUGLASS

MAKE THE GRADE

Narrative of the Life of Frederick Douglass came out in 1845. Frederick Douglass gave details about his time as an enslaved person that were unknown to many Americans at that time.

Autobiographies are often written by people who are famous, or well-known. Athletes, U.S. presidents, and **activists** have written some of the most successful autobiographies. President Bill Clinton put out his autobiography in 2004. It told about his life up through his presidency.

MAKE THE GRADE

Clinton's autobiography, called *My Life*, was nearly 1,000 pages long!

Many autobiographies are about the author overcoming adversity, or a hard situation. *Normal: One Kid's Extraordinary Journey* was written by Nathaniel Newman and his mom. They write about Nathaniel's health struggles and the many **surgeries** on his face and airways.

NATHANIEL NEWMAN (RIGHT) AND HIS FAMILY

MAKE THE GRADE

Autobiographies can be used as primary sources to help readers understand different ways of life, or cultures.

TYPES OF AUTOBIOGRAPHY

In a memoir, the author writes about one part or event of their life. They only cover a short period of time. This kind of autobiography may be written at any time in the author's life.

MAKE THE GRADE

Jacqueline Woodson's memoir *Brown Girl Dreaming* is about the author's childhood, including her awareness of the **civil rights movement**.

A personal essay can be a kind of autobiography too. While one essay is much shorter than a book-length autobiography, some people put many essays together to make up their autobiography. Each essay focuses on one topic, idea, or event in their life.

ALMA FLOR ADA

MAKE THE GRADE

Island Treasures: Growing Up in Cuba by Alma Flor Ada is a collection of essays and stories about her childhood growing up in Cuba.

Graphic novels can be autobiographies too! Often, the author also creates the cartoons, pictures, or other illustrations. *Relish: My Life in the Kitchen* is all about author Lucy Knisley's life and love of food. She wrote and drew the book.

MAKE THE GRADE

Authors who create the pictures in their autobiography further show how they saw themselves and the world around them.

Many autobiographies are written **intentionally**. Some are **compiled** from a person's letters or journals. *The Diary of a Young Girl by Anne Frank* came out in 1947. Her father had parts of her diary published after her death.

MAKE THE GRADE

Diary of a Young Girl includes what Anne wrote while her family was hiding from the German army during World War II (1939–1945).

VOICES FROM HISTORY

Autobiographies are an important primary source. They tell the story of history in the voice of those who lived it. Historians use autobiographies written during or about a time period to find out what life was like then.

MAKE THE GRADE

Reaching for the Moon: The Autobiography of NASA Mathematician Katherine Johnson teaches readers not only about Johnson, but also what it was like to be a woman working in the sciences in the mid-1900s.

Autobiographies are the best primary source to learn about a person. They include details about a person's life that wouldn't be known otherwise. The author is free to write exactly how something happened, how they felt, and what they think about it looking back.

MISTY COPELAND

MAKE THE GRADE

In *Life in Motion: An Unlikely Ballerina*, dancer Misty Copeland looks back on her journey to becoming a top ballerina.

YOUNG WRITERS

Even kids and teens write autobiographies! Jordan Romero's autobiography *No Summit Out of Sight: The True Story of the Youngest Person to Climb the Seven Summits* came out before he turned 19. Are you ready to write your story?

MAKE THE GRADE

Some autobiographies, like Romero's, are written with a co-author. This is often an **experienced** writer who helps shape the story of someone's life for readers.

USING AN AUTOBIOGRAPHY AS A PRIMARY SOURCE

Visit your local library to find an autobiography about someone you'd like to learn about. It can be a person from history, your favorite YouTuber, or someone totally new to you.

Read the book. As you read, decide what kind of autobiography it is: a traditional autobiography about the author's whole life, a memoir, or a collection of personal essays.

Once you've finished reading, answer the following questions:

- *At what point in their life did the author write their autobiography?*
- *Why did this person write their autobiography?*
- *What can it tell you about the time period they live or lived in?*

Look for more primary sources from the author. They may have created artwork, written letters, or posted a lot of videos on YouTube! Use these primary sources and the autobiography to write a short paragraph about what you learned about the author.

GLOSSARY

activist: One who acts strongly in support of or against an issue or cause.

author: A person who has written something.

civil rights movement: A time period in U.S. history starting in the 1950s in which Black Americans fought for equal civil rights, or the freedoms granted to us by law.

compile: To put pieces of writing together in a publication or collection.

detail: A small part of something.

event: A happening.

experienced: Having skill or knowledge from doing something.

intentional: Done in a way that is planned.

point of view: A way of looking at something.

surgery: A medical process in which a doctor cuts into the body to repair or remove something.

traditional: Having to do with long-practiced customs.

witness: To see something happen.

FOR MORE INFORMATION

BOOKS

Coyne, Kendall, and Estelle Laure. *As Fast as Her: Dream Big, Break Barriers, Achieve Success.* Grand Rapids, MI: Zondervan, 2022.

Yousafzai, Malala, and Sarah J. Robbins. *Malala: My Story of Standing Up for Girls' Rights (Abridged Edition).* New York, NY: Little, Brown Books for Young Readers, 2018.

WEBSITE

20 Best Autobiographies of All Time
www.rd.com/list/best-autobiographies/
Check out some of the most famous autobiographies out there.

Publisher's note to educators and parents: Our editors have carefully reviewed these websites to ensure that they are suitable for students. Many websites change frequently, however, and we cannot guarantee that a site's future contents will continue to meet our high standards of quality and educational value. Be advised that students should be closely supervised whenever they access the internet.

INDEX